growing wings

a view from inside the cocoon

The art and words of Kristen Jongen

Soul Soup Publishing, LLC, Traverse City, MI

Published by Soul Soup Publishing, LLC 109 S Union Street, Suite 202, Traverse City MI, 49684

Design and Layout by Robin Appleford 6661 Mathison Rd S, Traverse City, MI 49686

ISBN: 0-9773862-0-1

Printed in China

many thanks

Thank you to my children; Anya, Mia and Van. While appearing to make me

lose my mind, you may in fact have been the only thing holding me together.

I love you. To Mom, Dad, Talisa and Amy, what can I say? You breathed life

back into me when I couldn't breathe on my own.

Thank you to all of my friends, my sister and all the members of my family.

I hold you dearly.

Thanks to Robin Appleford for being my 24-hour sounding board and

amazing layout artist. The book is more beautiful than I ever expected.

Thank you for constant reassurance during the emotional transition it took

for me to write this book.

Thank you Kristina Stewart, for your steady confidence and for editing my

words in a way that is true to my voice, and to Kathryn Hack for her last

minute miracle edits.

Thank you Todd Jongen, whose support for this project speaks to the triumph

of integrity and courage... and the miracle of life's second act.

the children
constantly renovated
her heart

building larger rooms and revealing hidden chambers

they planted laughter
seeds in the carpet

and painted
wild flower Songs

that melted the Walls

This book is dedicated to Anya, a beautiful girl who has had her father and I spinning since the day she entered our world. Know that you are loved from every angle. Know that we are merely human. For thirteen years, your blue eyes have encouraged me to be a better woman. I pray that I will do you justice. I love you.

-Mom

Part she
...half he
a divine Manifestation
of God and grace
Singular combinations
of magic Stars
...and Moonbeams
"Sure to change the world
...never to be repeated

Contents

intro

Since starting Soul Soup, I have been honored with requests to write a

book. At first I imagined I would simply compile a catalog of my artwork

and poetry. EASY, right? Then I began adding snippets of articles and

writings here and there. My intention was to provide something thoughtful

and nourishing, perhaps wavering a bit and delving into some important

lessons I had learned. My eyes got misty with anticipation. I could already

hear the humming of rave reviews. "How could a girl her age be such an

old soul?" and "Her wisdom is uncanny." I was 150 pages away from my

first paper pulpit.

After years of pushing, my artwork was finally getting national attention.

Requests were rolling in. How about a line of handbags? Greeting cards?

It was fantastic! My marriage was stable. We had

seemingly overcome our toughest hurdles. We had

a history of intense love and struggle behind us.

Our first child was a surprise, born while we were

in college. I was 19 at the time. But we were the

lucky ones. We graduated and survived! After a

14-year, jagged climb, his job was promising and

our finances were comfortable. Things were finally

falling into place.

A book was going to be the next perfect step in

what was shaping up to be my newly-charmed life.

I didnt account for the universe and its plan

What a Shock!

As I started writing, things took a radical turn.

I started digging. I started searching. I started

waking up and telling the truth. My life quickly

unraveled into a not-so-impressive bowl of runny

JELL-O. The substance was questionable. At one

point I was forced to go deeper or literally die.

In essence, I am a completely different person

now than I was three years ago when I started

compiling my little book.

a whisper pierced the darkness of an obtuse slumber

the time is now... she beckoned

Awaken ©2005 Soul Soup

When she desperately clutched her dreams

they would often wiggle free and swim away

it wasn't until she learned to swim

that it became clear

. . . . . they were trying to show her the way. . . . .

This book has shaped itself into a tale of transformation. We often hear about the metamorphosis of a person but rarely see what life inside the cocoon looks like. It can be profoundly gruesome and intensely beautiful, all at the same time. This is a story of growing up, losing love, telling the truth and emerging through the death of a caterpillar... into a Butterfly.

If your life has taken unexpected U-turns, careened into complicated terrain or not gone according to the script you had written, my hope is this book will be a source of comfort and inspiration. I am here to tell you that what may appear to be the worst thing in your life could turn out to be the profound opening of your heart and your soul.

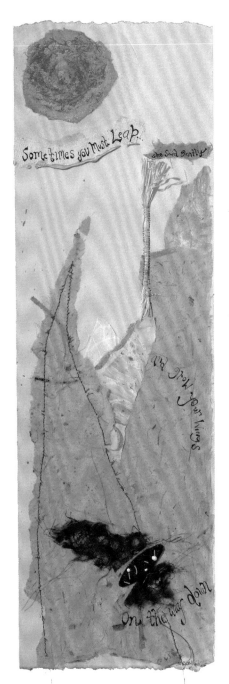

Sometimes you must Leap...
she said gently

try grow your wings

On the way down

Growing Wings ©2005 Soul Soup

I Have

learned this:

hold on Loosely

be prepared for anything
and accept that you will
still be unprepared for everything.

In this book, I *hope* you will gain strength in knowing you are exactly where you are supposed to be.

I pass a spirited baton on to you. With it comes the willingness to trust, to laugh, to learn, to be

vulnerable, to grieve and to choose love again. Most important, I hope this book inspires you to move

forward, knowing you are not alone. We are brothers and sisters in this miraculous journey called life.

We are all in this together. Namaste. your friend

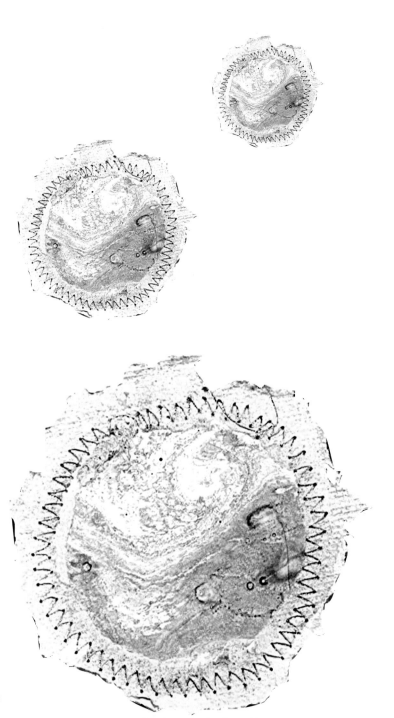

Journal, Feb 25 2004

Here I am. Fresh journal in hand. I

have been obsessing all day about the

anticipation of writing. I couldn't wait!

Per usual, as the time grew closer, I

started to get nervous, to panic.

Hours earlier, I had the perfect words. They bubbled so freely, scribbled on a napkin. I needed more space to

get it out. I wanted to explode. Thoughts, ideas and revelations spilled from the pump eloquently.

Now is my scheduled time to write: kids in bed, free time available. It has finally arrived and I want to bail out.

I am constipated with uncertainty. The blank pages stare accusingly at me.

I will sit here. I will breathe. I will simply start.

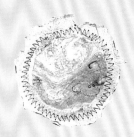

claiming truth

Several years ago, I was working with my life coach, Susan. Through her coaching process, I learned we

are encouraged to discover our code of light-who we are, who we were created to be. There is no striving

involved. It simply **is**. Throughout this process we journal and meditate and really dig into our past. Each

issue we talk about brings up particular words — words that, when reflected upon, make us realize we have

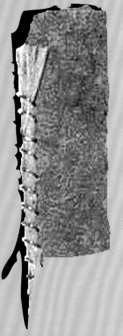

heard them throughout our lifetime in reference to ourselves. During one session I

had a breakthrough, a word coming to me consistently: "Truth." I knew that somehow

this word must be incorporated into my code of light. I shared it with Susan and she

reminded me to be aware of that word throughout my travels during the following

week. She told me about a client who claimed "Love" as part of her code of light and

was subsequently stuck in traffic for six hours next to a truck with that word printed on its side, all in capital letters. Looking out her window, for six hours, she was assured that Love was indeed part of her. The Tuesday night after my session with Susan, I went with a few of my girlfriends to an art show in Chicago. There were hundreds of booths of handmade work to salivate over. We were admiring metalwork when I spotted a sign above a booth that had my hometown of Traverse City, Michigan written on it. I bounded into the booth, anxious to meet the artist. I rarely met anyone in the city from my small hometown and was thrilled to connect. The artist made earth fairies of twigs, cloth and driftwood collected from the same beaches on which I grew up! I spotted a beautiful fairy right away and went to get a closer look. It was holding a small beach stone with a word lightly painted on it: Truth. I looked again. Shaking my head, I laughed and said to the artist, "Hey, that's my word."

She smiled, and gestured around the booth with her open hand. "That's my word too," she said. As I looked around, I saw dozens

Courtesy of Linda Chamberlain ©2003

of fairies lining the walls of her booth. Every one held a little stone. Every one said "Truth." I felt myself

circling around, doing a slow 360, like in a movie, out from a single camera shot into a wide-lens view. I

was surrounded by truth. There was only one isolated wood fairy that stood away from the crowd. Her stone

read "Hope." I know the truth has always been a part of me, but I started seeing it everywhere. I claimed it

as **my word**. I claimed it for my life. I privately committed to being a vessel of truth, and the universe heard

me. Its response was,

"it's time. Listen up, because the lessons are going to come Quickly."

and when your brilliant
Light is shining... she warned

Prepare to attract both the true... and the evil
the Latter is Low and Lean
...It finds Spirit's Achilles heel
...aiming to annihilate   the Soul and extinguish
the Light

...But the light,
she smiled

The Light of truth Cannot
be cloaked

It will radiate through the
eyes of her People

...It will dance off
the glass of her
seas

...It will illuminate
the blackest night Sky

and Faithfully
remind that
the Light... the light
always
outshines the
darkness

You will know
the truth. And
the truth will
set you free.

-The New Testament

One week later, my grandfather died.

Three weeks later, my husband, best friend and life partner of 14

years announced that he was unhappy. I didn't know what he meant,

but I tried to make a plan for us.

Three weeks after that,
I discovered he was in love with someone else.

One week after that,
I discovered I was pregnant with our third child.

My life quickly melted into a puddle of despair. This was the truth?

Was my enviable life a sham? What a horrible, rotten, unfair, cruel

trick! Where was the honor? One month later he moved out. Two

months later I broke my foot. Six months later I left Chicago for

good, on the verge of a nervous breakdown.

One year, many heartbreaks and many miracles later, I was living in a new state, a new town, a new house with a new office, driving a new car, loving a new baby boy and living a totally new life as a single woman and mother of three. My poetic work had changed. My messages were different. I know this is an extreme example, but it's absolutely feasible.

you can't fake authentic surrender

for it is the moment you unclench your hands... accept what IS and finally let go... that the fertile space is provided for divine intervention and unimaginable possibilities

Surrender ©2006 Soul Soup

I wont die
with my Song inside me
I sing everyday my eclectic tune
arms wide - raw heart exposed
I laugh as I make up words
knowing I will find my way
and persevere when my sweet song is reduced
to a raspy whisper
But I sing... Still I sing... Sing... Sing
My Song will not be caged
My radiant eyes will give it away
My Song has broad flowing wings that effortlessly Soar
and fill the sky
With wild colored Sprinkles of Me

My Song ©2005 Soul Soup

24

The moment I claimed the truth as mine, the universe took me seriously. Everything that wasn't authentic

began to fall away. Before any of this happened, if you had asked me what one thing I was certain of, I would

have answered confidently, "my marriage." So the truth came spilling out. The tiny holes became leaks that

were now gushing rivers. Any semblance of a foundation was washed away. It is only after intensive personal

work, therapy, and the grace of time that I am able to be this honest about what **is**. I spent many months

denying that what was happening was indeed related to my claiming the truth. It wasn't until later that I made

the connection between my truth and "that one isolated fairy": even amidst the most painful truths, there is

always room for hope. Not so ironically, hope is also a part of my code of light. My code of light is a spirited

life of radiant energy, raw emotion, truth-filled candor, sincere empathy and inspired hope.

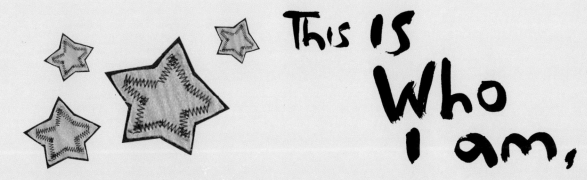

This IS Who I am,

naked and on
my knees
years of good enough
were callously
stripped away

an angel took mercy
and held my hand

...fear not my love
'good'
was merely insulating
you... from
vastly
great

Resurrection ©2005 Soul Soup

deconstruction

The Pickaxe

tear down this house. A hundred thousand new houses can be built from the transparent yellow carnelian buried beneath it. And the only way of getting to that is to do the work of demolishing and then digging under the foundation. With that value in hand, all the new construction will be done without effort. And anyway, sooner or later this house will fall on its own. The jewel treasure will be uncovered, but it won't be yours then. The buried wealth is your pay for doing the demolition.

-Rumi

There are times in everyone's life when the losses outweigh the gains, when despair is so great it is amazing we don't die from the pain. Sometimes we wish we could – it would hurt less.

During these radical times of desperation I have learned there is an opportunity. An opportunity to learn, an opportunity to be raw, an opportunity to listen and become the compassionate person we were meant to be. There are those who claim their loss or accident was the best thing that happened to them and we wonder, "How?"

Now I know. My most powerful lessons resulted from having faced my own crucifixion – felt it, witnessed it and died to the life I had before. I could not have resurrected stronger, and truer, without such a radical deconstruction.

If you are at a point in your life where darkness seems imminent, have faith. Breathe. Know there is light. This is not forever. Even in the darkest, most ominous room, it only takes a pinhole of light to pierce the shadows and eradicate the blackness.

Deconstruction means letting go of the struggle. It means accepting that there are times in our lives when we are merely human; flesh and bones capable of only so much. We must allow the stripping of our past selves, let every layer that isn't our truth fall away, and trust that a new life lies past this curve in the road.

Going Home ©2005 Soul Soup

Soul feet

"The condition of your feet represents the condition of your soul," my yoga teacher in Chicago was fond of saying. She recommended we massage our feet every night with ample amounts of lotion and never allow calluses to build.

Since I was a kid, there has been a direct correlation between my feet and stress. Often in a rush, I'll catch the corner of a door or the edge of something sitting right in front of me.

I distinctly remember when I was 14 and in a hurry to get to school, smashing my foot against a cast-iron radiator. I was barefoot.

I hobbled to the back room, stuffed my swollen right foot into a lace-up shoe and ran for the bus. It hurt, but I had things to do.

To this day, whenever a doctor sees my foot, he grimaces at the bent toe that reshaped itself into a modified right angle.

 The week my husband moved out, a solid wooden bench fell on my foot at a party. It was my first social event without him. Newly pregnant, I was an emotional disaster. Although it was painful, I stayed throughout the evening. The next morning, waking with intense pain, I saw the entire top of my foot had turned green. It was discolored from the base of my toes up to where my ankle started. I skipped getting an X-ray.

A few months later while the left foot was still healing, I twisted my ankle and fell flat on the sidewalk. I was primarily concerned with protecting my stomach. After three days, I surrendered and went to the emergency room. I had officially broken the other foot. I was to wear a removable cast for six weeks that looked like a clunky left shoe on a right foot. It was clumsy, and in it I couldn't walk fast.

balancing inner
and Outer
is a careful dance of dream speaking songs
and transparent truth bubbles
a two step that knows
when to kiss the ground
... and when to take flight

Balancing Act ©2005 Soul Soup

Unbeknownst to me, my friends placed bets on how long I would wear it. When I threw in the towel

ten days later my friend Jen exclaimed, "I won! I knew you wouldn't last two weeks!"

During the first 12 months of our separation I smashed several toes, had a perpetual string

of bruises atop both my feet, stepped on a fresh razor blade (that had to be extracted) and

broke my foot.

I wonder if the podiatric damage is directly related to the fact that I don't wear shoes?

I am always barefoot when my injuries occur

Wouldn't shoes help? I felt pride in my warrior's spirit; my tough side that pushed pain away and

did what needed doing. As I mature, I feel I am getting soft.

I wonder if I am simply Openhearted or terribly reckless with my Soul?

I am pondering this question as a stressful week winds down. I have been emotionally off-balance for a few days

and feeling shaky. I was reminded tonight to take it easy when I looked down at my bare foot, and was surprised

to see a new, apple-shaped bruise, forming on top.

I vaguely remember something dropping on it yesterday. Was it a large can of tomatoes? I can't recall. I was

unloading groceries, and ...

Now I am alone. I am lying on the couch. My foot is up and resting. I inspect the damage. Not bad visually. Cute

feet despite their abuse. The bruise is grey and tender. The cracked toenail from a previous incident has almost

completely grown out.

But in the pain department it is throbbing, and subtly breaks my heart. It gets my attention. I apologize for my

oafish behavior. I thank the little bones for taking me to so many places, for being so loyal and for not giving up

on me. I recognize they are brave for continuing to walk and run and even risk jumping. I get some ice. I am not

interested in stuffing my foot into a shoe. I want to be gentle with myself and caress the bruise away.

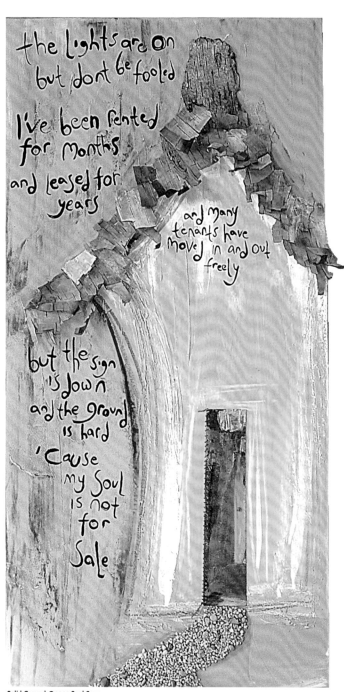

the lights are on
but dont be fooled

I've been rented
for months
and leased for
years

and many
tenants have
moved in and out
freely

but the sign
is down
and the ground
is hard

'Cause
my Soul
is not
for
Sale

Solid Ground ©2005 Soul Soup

demolition

Journal, Mar 24 2004

Thinking of demolition, it is a surreal parallel that I am literally living in a "tear-down" right now. My home has been

deemed a "tear-down" by the economics of our community. One-by-one the small houses are being bought by builders

and bulldozed. Demand to live downtown is heavy, and entire city blocks have been transformed in two short years. The

land has exceeded the value of the modest homes. The irony doesn't escape me.

My cute little cottage is 1,200 square feet. The lot it sits on is long and narrow, 50 by 188 feet. These homes are being

snatched up, demolished and monster mansions built in their place. 5,000 square-foot homes dominate the entire plat.

As I prepare to sell our home, I recognize a million-dollar mansion will take its place. I walk my kids to school

and am constantly faced with the running metaphor: Home after home, down for the count.

The house shells aren't merely knocked down, but completely unearthed. An entirely new footprint is dug, a

fresh foundation poured. It wouldn't make sense to leave a bathroom, or a standing staircase. It all has to go.

I feel like I am
being torn down
do I resist?
I look inward
I listen and hear a quiet whispering
"Let it go"
and I know that I must

My heart knows there is a blind spot in every leap of faith; a sheer panic as the last brick tumbles. At that moment, the space between life and death, the space in-between, is when we are completely vulnerable. There is nothing left except to completely surrender.

Maybe that's the point. Is it all about the honest and vulnerable surrender we must present in order to be re-built? The letting go of the fight? The letting go of the effects of the past, and the striving involved in the future? It can't be

rushed or faked.

Actively letting go

is the last straw of our

perceived human desire to control.

wrapping her arms around her torso
She held tight...to keep her heart from
falling out

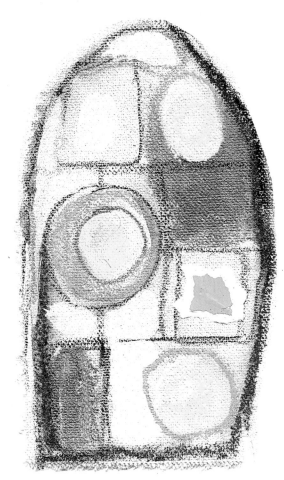

church

I have questioned whether or not to add this to the book,

because it seems so outrageous on top of everything else

during the deconstruction phase. But it is true.

Moving back to my
hometown WAS
A respite.
I felt safe
and protected

A few weeks after I moved back home I was driving through the downtown area of our city, running errands, very pregnant. I turned the corner of a familiar street lined with old traditional churches. Out of the corner of my eye I saw brown dirt on a vacant patch of land. I turned to look and my mouth dropped.

The historic Episcopalian church in which I had been raised was gone. It had been demolished. Nobody had warned me. I had to pull over and stop the car. There were backhoes and bulldozers kicking up dust in what used to be a treasure chest of wonderful memories. The most beautiful memory, of course, was the day I was married there.

I found out later the hundred-year-old stained glass panels, and many other historical elements that made Grace Church beautiful, had been saved.

Its in the
in-between

that
the real
magic
happens

the
seeds
are planted

the roots
take
hold

...and we
blossom
into who
we were
meant
to
be

Letting
go

It is okay to let go (in fact, it is required). I struggle greatly with this. I am a do-er, an act-fast kind of gal. In my

past life, my motto was DO IT NOW, all in caps. Have a great idea? DO IT NOW. Research it, work it, nurture it,

feed it, work it some more. Surround the idea with such an ominous presence that it doesn't have a chance to

escape and be unsuccessful or breathe. The first time I heard the phrase "let go and let God," it was a concept I

had never dreamt of. What about "never give up"? What happened to "hard work pays off"? The rules of success

I had clung to, all seemed to have a contradictory cousin. While my life was collapsing I spent many weekends

in Michigan trying to provide my children with a stabilizing force (my parents) while I fell completely apart.

Basic survival was my only goal and I neglected many responsibilities and commitments, including my beloved

garden back home in Chicago. My garden had previously been a source of pleasure. For five years I stood over it, watched it, protected, guarded and nursed each plant, willing it to grow. I convinced myself the only way my plants would thrive was from constant fretting and feeding. But now I surrendered to the realization that as the snow melted my garden would need to fend for itself. I simply couldn't nurture another living thing. I was exhausted and prepared myself for a summer of stalks and weeds. After returning from another impromptu visit to Michigan, it was late when my kids and I arrived back home in Chicago. We ambled through the back gate close to midnight. We had been gone for several weeks and I was looking forward to sleeping in my own bed. Sleepy kids, black lab and guinea pig in tow, we made our way through the yard. It was very dark outside and the full moon offered a crisp, steady glow.

Out of the corner of my eye, I was startled by a silky silhouette. I

took a closer look, and saw that it was a lavender Iris returning

from the year before. I squinted and looked closer and saw its

neighbors had returned also. I froze in amazement, dumbfounded.

Slowly I turned around and started to focus on other areas of

our property, and saw a yard full of blossoming plants. Thick,

heavy sprouts were popping up everywhere. Allium, Peonies and

Bleeding Hearts were green and lush. Hostas poked through the

Prayer
is like
that
she
whispered

Sometimes
it can
take
days
...Months
...years

and then
Sometimes
When I get
really
quiet

I can
see, hear
and feel
The answer
all at the
Same time

Prayer ©2005 Soul Soup

47

earth. Hyacinths were flowering. The yard was more beautiful that night than it had ever been. I stood

in the moonlight open-mouthed, with tears welling up in my eyes. My garden had grown on

its own. Standing in awe, I was profoundly aware of how closely the garden mirrored my life. I had

been supervising and forcing, bottle-feeding and staking-up many goals, dreams and relationships. I was

hyper-vigilant, afraid to miss a beat, afraid to trust. I would hover and strive and force things to work.

But I had disregarded one thing entirely – faith and the Master Gardener. Mothering had become my

M.O. Plants, it turns out, have a will to live. How incredible, how ironic that the plants had everything

they needed to not only survive on their own, but to thrive.

I had completely lost sight of the ultimate goal of the

universe: to nurture things and not try to live for them,

so they may in turn grow on their own; to sprinkle with

goodness, and let Mother Earth take care of the rest.

What a relief! What a gift! What a load off! When I feel

I am trying too hard, I picture the garden in my head,

and remember to simply sprinkle with love, let go and

let God do the rest.

This is an excerpt from one of my favorite books:

The Language of Letting Go by Melody Beattie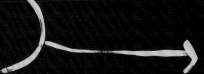

When I read the first two sentences,

I sat straight up in bed.

Letting Go, Dec 4

"How much do we need to let go of?" a friend asked one day.

"I'm not certain," I replied, "but maybe *everything*."

Letting go is a spiritual, emotional, mental and physical process, a sometimes mysterious metaphysical process of releasing to God and the universe that which we are clinging to so tightly.

We let go of our grasp on people, outcomes, ideas, feelings, wants, desires—everything. We let go of trying to control our progress in recovery. Yes, it's important to acknowledge and accept what we want and what we want to happen. But it's equally important to follow through by letting go.

Letting go is the action part of faith. It is a behavior that gives God and the universe permission to send us what we're meant to have.

Letting go means we acknowledge that hanging on so tightly isn't helping to solve the problem, change the person, or get the outcome we desire. It isn't helping *us*. In fact, we learn that hanging on often blocks us from what we want and need.

Who are we to say that things aren't happening exactly as they need to happen?

There is magic in letting go. Sometimes we get what we want soon after we let go. Sometimes it takes longer. Sometimes the specific outcome we desire doesn't happen. Something better does.

Letting go sets us free and connects us to our Source.

Letting go creates the optimum environment for the best possible outcomes and solutions.

The Language of Letting Go

- Melody Beattie

shoe drop

It occurred to me this reprieve of sadness is a choice. It's a choice to mentally let go of the obsession to worry even in the midst of the storm — and let the ship sail where it may. I am always afraid of retreating into denial if I don't face something down. Yet there is a happy medium, I suppose. A place where I choose to be optimistic. A place where I unabashedly allow myself freedom and happiness without feeling it's an invitation for the other shoe to drop. I want to learn to trust happiness. To let myself feel good. The shoe can drop whether or not I am happy, sad, pensive, obsessive, staring at it

or enjoying myself. Watching it drop is, in the end, no less painful than hearing it drop and turning to

look. Or hearing later that it has dropped. The fallout is the same. At least it has been, to this point.

Why not choose happiness?

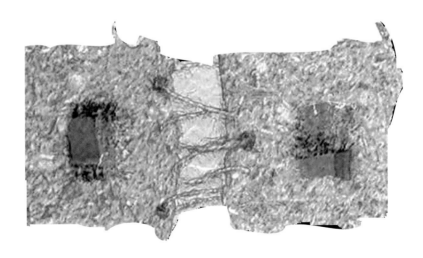

meditation

Please be with me today. I am afraid. Help me release this thing I cling to.

Help me let go in love.

Give me the wisdom and the peace to know you are in control and I can release my grasp.

I am OK. I am always OK.

I am ready to receive peace, peace, peace.

Perhaps Strength
doesn't reside in
having never been broken
...but in the Courage
required
to grow Strong
...in the
broken places

Strength ©2005 Soul Soup

butterfly

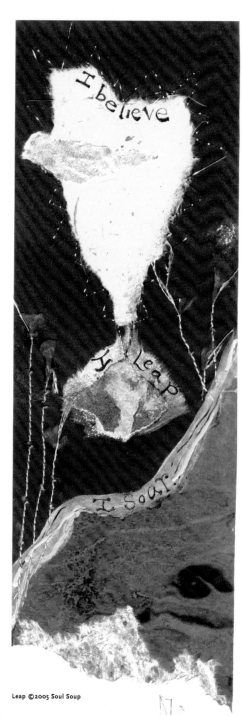

I believe

I Leap

I Soar

Journal, Feb 25 2004

I have been thinking a lot about butterflies. Stories and colorful images keep finding their way to me. I have always found butterflies beautiful, but the metaphor surrounding them a bit cliché. I've inwardly rolled my eyes at people who referred to themselves as "butterflies." I placed the reference on the "utterly un-profound" shelf with posters of fuzzy kittens and Valentine teddy bears.

Yet during this painful transition, the images keep appearing – in magazine articles, books, cards, stories, television. Butterflies keep making their way into my home. It all started with a quote from my friend Susan. I was in her office, sobbing uncontrollably. She quoted the end of her favorite story, gently interrupting me with "... and just when the caterpillar thought the world was coming to an end, it became a butterfly."

I wanted to be worthy of such a transformation. The crying ceased and I meditated on that thought. I hoped and prayed it was true.

I know within my heart that for a major metamorphosis to take place we are reduced to the jelly-like glob of non-caterpillar/ non-butterfly, an indescribable mass of nothing, hovering uncomfortably near death and yet profoundly, moments from rebirth.

What I have learned is the metamorphosis process is a choice. A caterpillar can remain a caterpillar for the entirety of its life, or it can risk the journey, totally deconstruct and have the faith that there are wings on the other side.

I can see very clearly that my past life is being stripped from me. I see myself becoming the jellied blob, hopefully on its way to a chrysalis.

I deeply mourn the stripping of my world. It is a profound loss as each layer of my caterpillar body, the life I cling to, is mercilessly peeled away, exposing raw, green skin. Every stripped layer brings me to my knees, bringing with it a fresh wave of sorrow, deeper than the last. Each time I hope it will stop there. But it continues. My heart has a sense that each layer is bringing me closer to my original core, the truth of who I am.

I am not a butterfly candidate... yet.

I cling to each caterpillar layer. Each has been excruciating in the letting go. At every level I have begged, "Dear God, let this be it!" and, "No, please not this..." Like a torn-off bandage on a sizeable wound, not a familiar strand of fuzz is left. The losses seem to come in a steady, insurmountable barrage; and yet somewhere deep inside, I know it all has to go. Everything caterpillar must end. I know this, and still it is hard to say goodbye.

Speechless ©2005 Soul Soup

During the shedding and stripping phase, while begging to save my one true thing, I become aware that my

"thing" is merely a human like me. I have invested in false gods. The idol I have manifested couldn't possibly

provide everything I require. It occurs to me the thing we cling to most often is the very thing needing desperately

to be released. It can also be the nail holding our feet to the floor. We are allowed to "pivot" on that nail, as Susan

pointed out, but we cannot even imagine flight. We grasp so hungrily onto our thing—job, relationship, children,

stuff, money—only to discover it is holding us back from freedom. Holding, squeezing, seizing and grasping are not

acts of love. They are acts of desperation and fear.

In faith, things ebb and flow. They breathe and radiate love. They are free to come and go.

babe

My eight year-old dog, Babe, is my companion. She is part Black Lab and part German Shepherd, with a

sprinkle of Chow and other various breeds. She is large and black and can look menacing. She is also my

best buddy. During the day she watches birds and squirrels from her perch on our porch couch. During the

evening she transfers to the front of the house, to wait for our resident raccoon to descend from the giant

maple in the yard. She barks, goes crazy and causes a ruckus. This is her daily routine.

When we go walking, Babe is impossible. No one wants to hold her leash. She pulls, she stops, she yanks.

Babe wants to do her own thing. I walk fast and like to think I am exercising. Babe will have none of it. The

moment she senses my heart rate might be rising above a slow drum beat, she stops, jerking my arm from

its socket.

Walking is my favorite form of exercise, but there is also a long history of discontent when others come along. With my kids, walking for exercise is a debacle. Someone has to go to the bathroom; a bike wheel breaks; someone is tired, thirsty, hot, cold-- you name it! Our walks are always cut short. Many of my friends can't keep up with my pace. I walk fast so, in consideration, I am forced to slow down.

during this time, the need
to walk at my own pace
is overwhelming

I have ditched everyone
....including Babe

A few nights ago the girls were with their Dad, the moon was out and it was a beautiful, balmy night. "Come

on, Babe," I called to my forlorn friend. She was ecstatic to be taken from exile.

Because it was so late, traffic was light. Parts of my walk are close to the road, but I didn't put Babe's leash

on. She was able to cruise freely, and I wondered if I was inviting disaster. She sniffed a bit when we started

off but I continued to walk. Then she trotted up next to me. She stayed close to my left side, and even trotted

a step ahead of me. I had to broaden my step to keep up with her. It was a bit faster than I would normally

push myself. My heart was beating fast and it felt great.

I laughed at the irony and asked, "Babe, could it be that you are the perfect walking partner after all?"

Perhaps she is more like me than I knew.
She can more than keep up.
She just refuses to be on a leash.

waiting it out

bodies full of grace
Bellies full of life
eyes filled with soul

the
worlds
great
healers
call
themselves
. . . . SHE

The She's III ©2005 Soul Soup

Journal, April 2 2004

My newest plan is to simply wait it out. Beat it with tenacity. I have a goal of five months (when the baby is due). My plan is to take the next five months to heal. I have already put in four (albeit the worst four months of my life). But in five months it will be total of nine months, and surely I will be in a better place. My goal is to be happier and to welcome my new baby in peace and love. So I will wait it out.

On my daily meltdown I will remind myself that I am one day closer to light. I will let myself cry, cry hard like I have been, but with the intention of getting it all out. I will watch chick-flicks and comedies and basically pass the time. I won't be perfect. I have 14 years of memories to sift through. I will cry more. I will write and wait in an attempt to let go. I will socialize and be uncomfortable on my new single legs. I will cry again. But in five months, five short months, it will be easier. It has to be.

Some days...

IN AN
Effort
to pull
at least
ONE
thing
together

Lipstick
..WAS
ALL SHe
could
do...

Lipstick

©K.Gorger

Lipstick©2005 Soul Soup

I will move forward step by painful step and make scary decisions and cry some more. I will hold on too tightly again, I am sure, and be needy and inappropriate at times and take many steps backwards. I won't strategize with my emotions. I won't play games. I won't lie. I will be painfully honest about where I am. My goal is real healing. My goal is letting go in love. I will not call. I will not solicit one more trauma. I will practice paying attention to myself and give my kids the mental space this thing is currently occupying. I will slowly stop obsessing. There will be days ahead when I don't feel this pain at all. There will be moments when I forget to be sad. Until then, I will wait it out.

P.S. I usually believe that "the journey is the destination," but in this case I am not that highly evolved. As of right now, this journey sucks.

friends

It was the 'She's' who saved her
pulled her up

they wore A lifetime blanket
of old + wise

And pulled her through

greent blessed
truths

that Cradled
her soul

and saved her
from
freezing

Journal, Dec 31 2004

So many miraculous discoveries keep arriving. The most surprising is the amount of love that is sprouting up around me. I am afraid to put it into words, because I don't think I can do it justice. The sensation is beautiful and utterly surreal.

The irony is unsettling. I feel as if I have been grasping at love for a long time. Encircling it; trying to round up its contents and convince it to stay. All of my focus was in one direction. Grasping at crumbs and creating imaginary meals, I couldn't (or wouldn't) receive it from a place of abundance. Looking from the outside, the energy I was using to get love from where it was unavailable, was a deflector from the vast open sources that were ready and willing.

the She's were like that...
they had their own language

Nods, glances.
...smirks
and mischevious
winks

they wielded
their powers
with great
restraint

.....but unleashed love
like the mighty

The She's II ©2005 Soul Soup

In her darkest hour
The She's
emerged like
clusters of stars
singing and dancing
holding up the sky

with
their
healing
illumination

The She's IV ©2005 Soul Soup

As one desperate love makes a hasty withdrawal, a brighter, more quiet force surrounds me. It feels different. It feels whole and nurturing; steady and filling. I am insulated by a consistent energy that is represented in dozens of familiar faces. My friends and family surround me with padding and cushions; with words so filled with strength, I feel overwhelmed by support.

I honestly never knew
such love existed in the world
Let alone for me.

Vulnerability is something I have never worn with ease. It was more gratifying to be the strong one, the one with

answers. My friends came to **me** for advice. My ego enjoyed its space. Being the giver allowed me to be in control.

It put me in the driver's seat.

I am not prepared to be so broken now. My hearty attempts to hide a shame-filled nightmare are not persisting.

It takes every ounce of energy I can muster to merely breathe. And yet, the soft spot I so readily cover is turning

out to be my ultimate salvation.

because, she said smiling

..you are my friend

My Friend ©2005 Soul Soup

This week the words keep spilling free from the strangest places, from the most unexpected people. Many friendships I relish are brought to a new level. Acquaintances I honored have developed into deepening connections. Three words that have been previously set aside for special occasions are expressed freely and without reserve. My girlfriends, yoga teachers, old college roommates, aunts, uncles, in-laws, parents, sister and colleagues have been moved to reach out. They give intense hugs, hold my hand, send cards and leave messages on my answering machine simply saying "I love you."

I Like myself

Every summer for the past 10 years my children have spent two

weeks in July with their paternal grandparents in New York. The visits

started with just Anya, but as our family grew, so did the cluster of

children making their way east.

During that year of seperation, my life had tipped into a state of

unbalance. I was still grasping at being a single mom. I had my hands

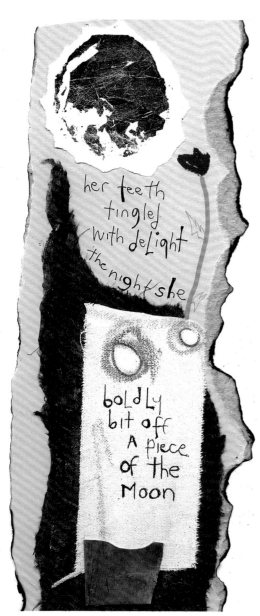

her teeth tingles with deLight the night she boldly bit off A piece of the Moon

New Moon ©2005 Soul Soup

full, so instead of cleaning the garage or working longer hours while

the kids were scheduled to be gone, my girlfriend and I decided to

take full advantage of our free time and our frequent-flier miles. I

asked several of my well-traveled friends for advice, and we chose

Bali because of the artistic and religious nature of the island. With a

three-day stopover in Hong Kong, our trip would be just shy of three

weeks. We scheduled our trip six months in advance, but a few weeks

later my travel buddy Talisa had to cancel. In the fervor of opening

her new business she was unable to

commit to such an extended leave.

I understood her dilemma and set

my disappointment aside.

Without hesitation, I trusted divine

timing and decided to go it alone.

I have been on short business trips

and spent a few nights in hotels here

I am enough
I have
enough
I love
enough
I risk
enough
I fill enough
I get enough
I handle enough
I am loved enough
I am healed enough
I am ready enough
I am enough

Enough ©2005 Soul Soup

and there, but wouldn't consider myself a seasoned independent traveler. Yet at no time did I fret or worry. A travel agent set the whole thing up, added a few tours and customized some outings. There was too much going on in my life to actually think about the impending trip... my chance for escape!

Much of the time, I felt like I was wearing a suit of armor just to get through the day. I was afraid of becoming too tough and jaded. I spent my days barking orders at the kids or negotiating fees with faceless customer service reps. I made expensive decisions on my own that stressed me out. I navigated unsteady terrain on fairly wobbly legs. I worried that I was slipping into the dreaded role of "bitch."

It wasn't until I was actually sitting

getting
quiet
is always
good

In the Stillness
clarity emerges

in the breath
the answers
reveal themselves

and in the
in between

there is
Peace

it's really
Quite Simple

I believe

....in You

Simple ©2005 Soul Soup

in the 747 in O'Hare airport, the kids securely with their dad,

the house locked up and the pets accounted for that I laughed,

and asked out loud, "What am I doing?" Sitting there in my

seat, my usual uniform of anxiety and tension started to melt.

Without anyone vying for my attention, I peacefully read my

book and smiled to myself, excited for the first time.

Traveling alone, my defenses were down. I had to stand in my

own shoes and move about the world hailing cabs, checking

in and out of hotels; ordering and tipping; socializing and

making friends. I was navigating by myself, with no kids to

hide behind. There were no roles or advantages of reputation to pad the way. I was simply a mid-30's single American female traveling alone.

On one occasion, a shop owner referred to me as the "crazy white woman." I mused, "that was probably the most appropriate assertation of all of my roles."

In 32 years I have had a wide range of experiences. And yet in 32 years, I had never spent so much time alone. What a beautiful gift! There were times I was desperate for simple conversation, and at times I grew tired of the rambling of a new companion and yearned for silence. But mostly I was able to see my spiritual self on a worldly level not attached to any of my gathered roles: Kristen the mom, daughter, ex-wife, friend, boss, lover, artist, business-owner, client, patient, student, neighbor, activist, teacher, co-signer, borrower, lender... what freedom!

By myself, I had the chance to be quiet. No longer frazzled and running late, the fanfare and drama that usually followed me disappeared. I was responsible only for myself. I saw myself from the outside. I didn't

feel the angst and self-consciousness that had plagued my adolescence. I felt quietly confident.

I laughed easily with new friends, sans the nervous giggle. I had heartfelt talks with my guides and learned

what it means to be Hindu. I participated in a three-day Hindu festival wearing a sarong and sash, honoring

Wisnu, the God of protection and water. I attended a funeral and outdoor cremation. I was invited into

homes of villagers and met many beautiful children.

I made it a point to enjoy being with myself. For the first time in my life, I liked what I saw. My relentless

inner-critic appeared to be on vacation too. On occasions when I discovered myself "acting" a familiar stale

character, I gently let go and thought, "I am proud of that girl. She is doing her best."

I always expected to meet someone. I imagined for six months prior that I would not go alone. I thought one of my friends would hop on board at the last minute, or I would meet someone while abroad. I even fancied the idea of meeting an international lover. I didn't fret, because I knew with certainty I wouldn't be alone.

What I didn't know was the person I would meet was better than my fantasies. The person I met after 32 years of searching...

was **myself**.

In Bali I met a girl with whom I truly connected; a girl I respected and admired; a girl I liked being around, who made me laugh. We now talk daily, and she feels the same way. She reminds me of how fun I can be. When my tension uniform becomes too tight, she tells me I am beautiful and reminds me to breathe.

breathe

Courage

is a quality I have always admired. I've been told I'm "strong"

and "courageous" for as long as I can remember. My candor comes off as courage. People have even said to

me, "Well, it's easy for you," as if somehow, confrontation is easy. I have always wanted to be a courageous

person. It is much more difficult than it looks.

In the movies, we see quick-witted people with great comeback lines, people who stand up to others without

even blinking. In real life, many times we think of a good comeback three days later, or wish we had spoken

up. We berate ourselves for being cowardly.

As I seek maturity, I'm keenly aware of how much courage

it takes to be the woman I want to become. I'm faced

with many situations from which I want to run. I have

been practicing getting quiet, taking a deep breath and

moving steadily into the truth, instead of avoiding it. It is

terrifying. Sometimes truth comes out jagged, or blunt. I

might cry or don't know what to do. Since claiming my truth

two years ago I've had more uncomfortable conversations

than I have had in the sum of 32 years. I am not looking

Courage doesn't always roar. Sometimes courage is the quiet voice at the end of the day, saying I will try again tomorrow.

—Mary Anne Radmacher

for trouble! Is the universe is testing me? "You said you want to be a beacon of truth? Let's see how

you do on this." And, "Oh, here's a good one, she's sure to run now." I am still tempted to jump out

my office window rather than deal with a pending situation, but it *is* getting better. It *is* getting easier.

I have learned so many things about courage. For me, it is rarely chest-beating. It takes many shapes.

It can be standing up for something that is wrong; it is an opportunity to be myself, to express what I

am really thinking and feeling. It is addressing painful situations with compassion. It is the strength to

look a dark secret in the eye. It is the willingness to express my vulnerability to people I fear the most.

It is calling someone I have hurt and explaining that things didn't come out right and sincerely apologizing.

It is courage that allows me to begin telling the truth; it takes

courage to be vulnerable, courage to admit ignorance, courage

to be the girl who doesn't know anything, but is willing to learn.

It is the courage to...

tell my friends that I love them.

to walk into Weight Watchers, get on a scale and admit what I have been doing to my body.

look in my recycling bin and count the wine bottles.

show my newest artwork to a gallery owner, or maybe even simply a friend and to try again, when it is rejected or misunderstood.

to say "this is me," and to stand there.

move forward, when the past is not totally resolved.

let my kids be themselves, when I don't understand. It is the courage to let them grow.

hold on to my spirit.

let a person go, when they need space.

open up a high stack of overdue bills, and start making phone calls.

pay attention to my mate, and recognize strange behavior.

take the blinders off.

recognize my own strange behavior.

not to laugh, when I have been offended.

to say, "How can I help?"

stop and help someone in need.

say no.

And most importantly I work on the profound and absolute courage it takes to move forward

... and to say yes.

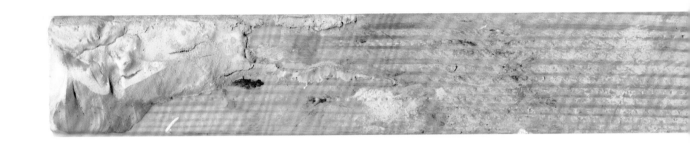

I Pray every morning for Courage
the courage to stand
in that space
even if my knees
are knocking
and fill my own
shoes

miracles

Miracles come in many obscure moments and the pulsing places in between. I've spent much of my life awaiting my big break. I didn't know what it was. I just knew that it would save me. From what, It didn't matter. I thought miracles would be third-person experiences gifted to me when I was worthy enough. I desperately searched with my eyes wide open. I grasped onto passing thoughts. I started businesses with the idea that 'this might be it!' I held onto friendships with a frenzy, and men with a silent desperation. I would rather be dragged down the street, my white knuckles attached to a speeding potential, than risk missing something. "Slow Down, you are my miracle!!" I saw myself shouting through the exhaust.

I expected my miracle to be the enlightened version of a red Ferrari.

Her Miracle
came Unannounced
...and in an odd
package

It looked different than She had Imagined

UnPolished

Untimely

Unexpected

.....Unpretentious...

...yet it fit perfectly

divinely Constructed
Solely
For her

It would come to my house, bang on the door and exclaim, "Hello Kristen, I am your miracle. Consider yourself discovered. I am here to change your life." Of course I would recognize it. It would be wearing a name tag: Occupation Miracle #1, or Financial Miracle #2, or the ever-impressive Stud Miracle #3. You see, I didn't know what to do with my life. I was confused and praying for answers. I ran anxiously to the mailbox, checked email compulsively and read "How-to" books. I was afraid to let a potential moment slip by. I thought the answers would be coming from the outside.

A lot of living has taught me the opposite is true. Upon taking inventory of my miraculous life, I've discovered all of my miracles have been divinely sent, without fanfare. Many, I am ashamed to admit, I blew off entirely. I was too busy looking past the person in front of me—daydreaming on the "maybe," while tripping over the "real deal." No miracles came to the front door. Some came to the back door and knocked for awhile. A small few dropped in from the sky. Many were in the room with me the entire time, simply waiting for me to notice.

All, however, have been a perfect fit. My writing is a miracle. For years I was chasing down my career. I wanted to be a designer of any kind. I had ten businesses, but never the words. They were there, waiting, but I wasn't listening. With a little time and patience, it now appears the words that **have me.**

Miracles have manifested in unplanned children who were perfectly timed; in awkward job offers that colored a bizarre brick road; odd moves across the country. They appeared in strange interactions that placed me squarely in front of new, best friends. Miracles disguised as disasters that were the groundwork for unbelievable resurrections.

they all have one thing in COMMON

They were not orchestrated by me.

God was in charge. The motivating engine wasn't my panic. I wasn't forcing, clinging or manipulating. Half the time, I wasn't even paying attention. The doors flung off their hinges and the road paved itself. I just committed to showing up.

I committed to being present and letting go; the action part of faith.

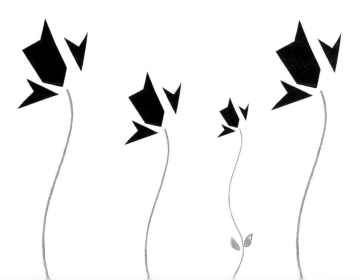

With years came Courage
and they finally faced off

She and herself... herself and She

eye to eye
they looked
eachother Over...

Sized eachother UP...
and cried enough For Two

She ultimately Noticed herself as Gentle and Kind

Herself decided forgiveness

was deserving of she

forgiveness

the space
inbetween us
is saturated with
    clutter
past lives . growing buds
sleeping dreams and
        hidden hopes
all steal our attention
            from now

Love waits making it difficult
to know what to say

Love Waits ©2005 Soul Soup

At a recent conference, one of the speakers was the father of a young boy who had been murdered. He was a beautiful, compassionate man who was clearly struggling with the loss of his first born. As part of his recovery, he was working with the shooter's grandfather to grieve and somehow make sense of this senseless act. After the conference, I told my friend how moved I was by his grace. My friend responded by saying, "I'm afraid I would never be able to forgive something like that."

I understood her dilemma. at one time in my life I feared the same thing.

What my friend didn't realize, is in moments of total despair:

The black pit of hatred makes it worse.

It is like gasoline on a fire.

Sometimes to forgive isn't an act of compassion, but merely self-preservation. A prayer that pleads "God please help me to release this pain," is answered with an inner knowledge that clinging to the darkness, pointing fingers, being embroiled in rage, isn't changing anything. The person isn't coming back, the tragedy isn't correcting itself. The only thing that is changing is the intensity of your misery. Worse and more painful than hating someone else, is unmercifully hating yourself. But misery can ignite miracles, so in order to live, you look desperately for solutions. You become willing to try anything, including the possibility of forgiveness.

...It's About
Big Love'
she professed
and letting go...
and bulging vulnerable
hearts
...and the honest truth
And the profound choice we
make everyday
to Live Our Lives
in Color
and choose
LOVE
again

Big Love ©2005 Soul Soup

I remember the first time I had that conversation with myself.

I was in wretched pain, sobbing as I drove down an Illinois highway, praying for peace. A voice in my head suggested that I consider the idea of forgiveness. "No way," I silently shouted so loud my skull rattled. I was furious at the thought. I was angry, bitter, sad, judgmental, lonely, self-righteous, withholding and totally toxic. "I won't give this up," I thought... and then instantly caught myself. "Just what would you be giving up?" asked my subconscious. Tears still streaming down my face, I laughed at my insanity. I admitted aloud, "Anger, bitterness, sadness, judgment, loneliness, self-rightousness, a fervor to withhold love and total toxicity." What would I get in return?

Peace.

hmmm...
it felt risky.

When the pain becomes great enough,
you take the risk.

It becomes clear that you must change Something, or die.

So you Consider.
You look from different angles.
you ask for help.

You admit that you
are afraid,
and you take a leap of faith.

You become willing to
Let go.

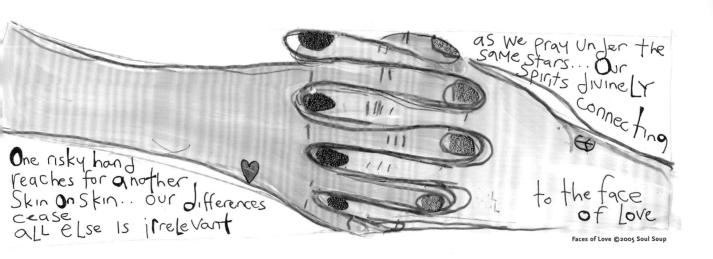

One risky hand reaches for another Skin on skin.. our differences cease all else is irrelevant

as we pray under the same stars... our spirits divinely connecting

to the face of Love

Faces of Love ©2005 Soul Soup

The world looks different, quickly. Your prayers are answered. Your heart is magnified. You develop more empathy for all those who have suffered before, realizing there are victims on both sides of the situation. You start becoming the kind of compassionate human being you never thought possible. You recognize suffering in a palpable way and begin to see the seed of humanity that unites us.

I hope my friend is spared that kind of grief. I pray she never has to experience it. I would not wish it upon anyone I love. And yet I know with confidence that if she does, she will find a side of herself she doesn't know exists. She will meet a person she didn't know who lives inside of her; a compassionate woman with a larger heart than she imagined. A person capable of unconditional forgiveness.

angeLs

My best friend Talisa is a healer, life coach and a spiritual intuitive.

She is not only my best gal pal, but my sister in many ways. She has

helped me through so much of my healing. Having gone through

a divorce one year prior to mine, she'd navigated terrain I hadn't

encountered. We talk for hours, and hold each other's virtual hands

on our bumpy trail. (Note: Once I was calling the phone company

to clear up my bill, and the lady on the other end said, "Girl, you

better keep your unlimited long distance plan. Obviously someone

very important to you lives in Chicago." I laughed as she rattled off

dozens of 300- to 400-minute calls to the 815 area code. "That's my best friend," I told her. "Mmm, hmm," she muttered. "Only one thing can keep a conversation going that long... and that's some man,"

I am blessed and graced by God with Talisa's friendshi,

Two years after leaving, I am in Chicago visiting Talisa's beautiful New Age bookstore, "Peaceful Inspirations."

The store is warm and the energy is loving. When I'm in town I can't wait to go there and simply hang out.

We talk and I pretend I am going to help out, but mostly I get enraptured in dozens of fabulous books; I curl

up on her cozy couch, read and drink tea. I'd only just arrived, when an eccentric-looking man with wild hair

and a trench coat began talking to Talisa. He was a spiritual medium giving her a reading. (Later I found

out the fascinating truths he revealed to her.) He turned to me as I walked through the door; his eyes were

wide as he said to her, "She is surrounded by angels." I laughed nervously and kept walking. He said, "I am

serious, there are angels all around you." I stopped walking and turned to him. He continued, "Your light

energy is drawing them to you." In that moment, I melted. I stopped my suspicious mind and thanked him. I didn't care if it was true or not. His assumption that I carried a radiant light filled me with gratitude for being treated to this wonderful vision.

Many miraculous things happen at Peaceful Inspirations. People often have intuitive thoughts and are moved to tears simply by being in Talisa's peaceful and accepting presence.

It feels like home. When visiting there, I keep getting a vision that my healing is coming full circle. Wings fill my head. "The time is now," it says. "The time is now." I finally tell Talisa I keep getting this message, and I know what it means; I just don't know what to do. My compulsive "action" requirement is activated and restless. She suggests I relax, and perhaps do nothing. We do a reading with intuitive OH! Cards, and my card reveals a locked door with a key in it. I know I have the key. **I know I am ready to open the door.**

We discussed my career, I was negotiating a potential contract with a greeting card distribution company. The invitation to join their line had been out of the blue. In my personal life, I'd just met an exhilarating man for whom I felt strongly. All of these things were exciting and frightening and happening fast, all at the same time.

So we sat on the floor and drank tea and talked. We both did a final reading and drew archangel oracle cards (angel cards have a deck of about 50 cards with various angels and their particular inspiration and order of protection). We spread them out on the table upside down and each picked one. Talisa picked her card, and we discussed the relevance in her life. It was the angel of rest. (I saw the relevance, even if she didn't!) I picked a card that got my attention and flipped it over. It was the archangel Ariel. My mouth dropped. I turned the card for her to see. Her mouth dropped too. It read,

Spread your wings. Do not hold back right now.

the timing is Perfect and You are ready to Soar!

My eyes filled with tears.

I signed the greeting card contract, and went for it with the dude.

Mia and the dragonfly

Journal, June 27 2005

I was at the beach tonight in the steamy 94 degree weather, with all three of my kids. Anya, 12, and Mia, 7, were

playing in the water while Van, 10 months, shoveled fistfuls of sand into his mouth. We were alone in a little private

cove aside from the main beach. Intermittently, I read a book and vainly tried to keep my naked, sandy baby from

eating stones. My book was hysterical, so I laughed out loud in random bursts and enjoyed feeling giddy for a change.

Mia came in from swimming, holding a pathetic-looking friend. A soggy dragonfly was on her outstretched palm. "Look Mama," she gasped. "He almost drowned." I obligingly stopped reading and looked up. "Mmm... hmm," I muttered. "I think his wings are wet," was all I could muster as I went back to find my place on the page, hoping to get five minutes of peace without interruption.

The heat besieged me eventually – the baby was cleaned off and finishing a bottle; Anya was looking for shells on the beach; I stood to take a quick dip and cool off. Out of the corner of my eye, I saw Mia.

Mia, mid-rescue

She was crouched down near some brush and boulders about twenty yards away whispering quietly. I watched her intently, trying to figure out what she was doing. When I did, I stopped dead in my tracks. She was talking to her dragonfly friend, who was resting on a rock. It had been more than a half hour since I had passively shrugged off her rescue.

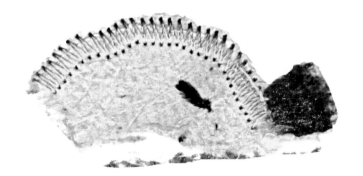

My world hadn't
seen her coming

the heart
on her sleeve
as big as Texas

She cries big
and Loves hard

and sings like it's the
only answer

...and in her Presence
my heart
sings too.

...and believes it is

Mia ©2005 Soul Soup

108

The sight of her brought immediate tears to my eyes. She cooed and sweetly sang to the little critter she believed in. I thought of how lucky that little bug was. He had no idea what a compassionate champion was rooting for him. The love that surrounded that girl's heart had electrified many rooms. She was hot and red and passionate and temperamental and had four temper tantrums a day since the day she was born.

She loves so big it hurts.

I thought how we could all use a Mia in our lives. Someone to see us drowning and simply scoop us up without a fuss. Someone to gently blow on our soggy wings and patiently encourage us to fly. My girl looked holy in that moment, and as I quietly watched her, I felt I was in the presence of God.

I walked out into the water and turned to look back at her, tears still in my eyes. She saw me and called out excitedly, "Look, Mama, look... his wings are moving!" I watched, simultaneously choking on tears and laughing with delight- as her lucky friend raised his laced wings and gracefully took flight.

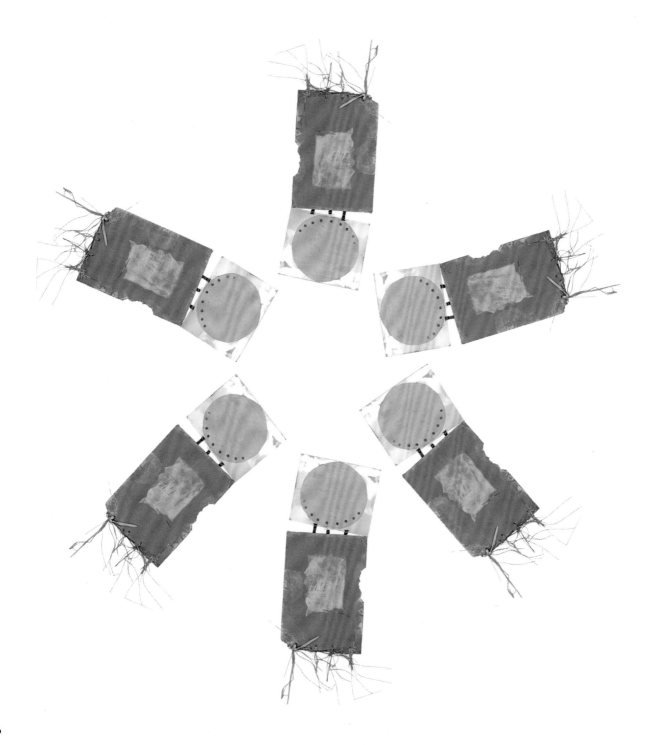

my tribe

I was talking to a friend on the phone one night. We were discussing being divorced, and the delicate art of single

parenting. I was telling him how heavily I had come to rely on my Mom and Dad in such a short time, since moving to

Michigan. "We all need a family," I was saying. "We need more than a family," he said. "What we need is a tribe".

A tribe. I love that word, "tribe."

It resonated heavily with me. The word conjured up the most nourishing imagery. A tribe is meatier than a village,

thicker than family and deeper than friendship. It is a group of people who have your back. People ranging in ages on

every rung of the ladder. Elders who give wise advice, adults who are thick as thieves, teenagers looked after with a close

eye, and children who are fiercely protected. A tribe can even consist of past spouses who know you better than anyone

else. It is a root system that is deep.

Same garden

Same garden, two years later...

I was back in Chicago for a visit. Talisa and I sat on a wooden bench under a thick, ivy-covered trellis speckled with violet Morning Glories. Our sanctuary was in the same place where the moonlit Iris had been two years before. The garden had grown into an impressive group of substantial flowering perennials, which she claimed had my energy.

We sat side by side, completely different people than we were when we met six years earlier. We started off as stay-at-home moms. Now there was me, with my surprising career as a writer and artist; and Talisa, a life coach with her own spiritual bookstore. We'd been through painful divorces exactly one year apart. As the sun began to set, I noticed a pair of Monarch butterflies dancing around and in between us, fluttering through the flowers that draped the trellis. I watched them, thinking about their visual significance.

the metamorphosis
was dramatic

the wings did appear

Perhaps,

now it is time to fly?

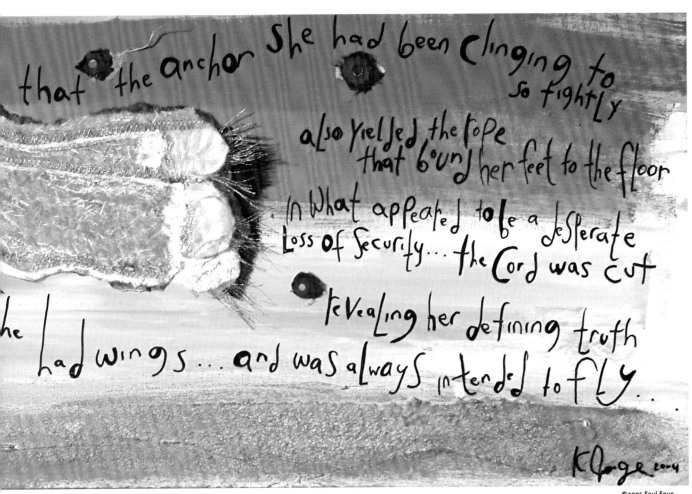

that the anchor she had been clinging to so tightly also yielded the rope that bound her feet to the floor. In what appeared to be a desperate loss of security... the cord was cut revealing her defining truth she had wings... and was always intended to fly...

KGoge 2004

I do not know whether I was then a man dreaming I was a butterfly. Or whether I am now a butterfly dreaming I am a man.

-Chuang Tzu

Acknowledgements

The inspiration for my poetry comes from many sources. The vast majority comes from a deep and knowing space. It simmers beneath the surface and reveals itself in unpredictable bursts. A handful of pieces were inspired directly by conversations I've had with my incredibly insightful friends, people whom I lovingly refer to as, "My Tribe."

"Growing Wings" is one of my very first poems. It was inspired by a phone conversation I had with my cousin Kari. She was referring to growing her wings "on the way down."

"Truth" comes from a conversation I had with my dear friend Talisa at 3:00 in the morning. While she didn't speak those words, it is the essence of what I heard in that profound moment.

"Strength" was inspired by a phrase from my friend Susan She would often refer to "being strong in broken places."

"My Song" was inspired with a lecture I heard by Dr. Wayne Dyer. He referenced "dying with your song inside" and it stuck with me for many years.

Page 83 Courage Copyright, Mary Anne Radmacher. Maryanneradmacher.com

Page 51 The Language of letting Go, Melody Beattie

Page 105 Archangel oracle cards, copyright Doreen Virtue P.H.D. AngelTherapy.com

Page 27 The Pickaxe, The Essential Rumi

Page 19 Artwork by Linda Chamberlain. lchamberlain.com

Other great sites: peacefulinspirations.com, ponderingpool.com, thepeacealliance.org, dopcampaign.org

View Kristen Jongen's entire portfolio @ mysoulsoup.com